250

D1281819

The War of
the Secret Agents
and Other Poems

The War of
the Secret Agents
and Other Poems

HENRI COULETTE

Charles Scribner's Sons · New York

Some of these poems have appeared in the following: *The Hallmark Book of World Verse* (Doubleday), *Homage to Baudelaire* (Cummington Press), *Hudson Review, International Literary Annual,* No. 2 (Criterion), *Mademoiselle, Midland* (Random House), *New Campus Writing* (Bantam), *New Poets of England and America,* First and Second Selections (Meridian), *New World Writing, Paris Review, Statement, The Literary Review.* "The Black Angel," "The Junk Shop" and "The Sickness of Friends" first appeared in *The New Yorker.* Copyright © 1963, 1961, 1964 The New Yorker Magazine, Inc.

Printed in the United States of America
Library of Congress Catalog Card Number 66-13336

For Jackie

This book is the Lamont Poetry Selection for 1965. The award, made annually by The Academy of American Poets, goes to a first book of poems by an American poet, selected by a panel of judges. For the 1965 contest the judges were: James Dickey, Anthony Hecht, Louis Simpson, W. D. Snodgrass and May Swenson.

Contents

I The Junk Shop

"The surprise was that there was nothing there,
Nothing at all, nothing, not even ought,
And thus it was that in my 35th year
I learned that by these words I hid my thought."

PHILIP LEVINE

Intaglio

I have a picture in my room in which
Four gawky children strike a pose and stare
Out at the world without a worldly care.
Three girls and a boy in a paper hat:
The one too much a mouse to be a bitch,
The bitch, the actress, and the acrobat.

The roles I give them, half suggested by
The poses that they took, are meaningless,
For they are playing games. It is recess
Or summer—we have interrupted them.
They pose for us, with Agile romping by
And dark-eyed Pensive plucking at her hem.

This is my family. I dust them now
And then, and they return the courtesy
By never growing up. Thus, irony
Becomes a kind of family likeness, treasured
Not for the casual sameness of a brow
But for the attitudes one's mind has measured.

I knew an Agile once. To prove himself
The nimbler one, he pushed his books aside,
And crossed to Europe and the war, and died,
And his agility, which I believed a power
Then, then was gone, and his books on my shelf
Harvest the sunlit dust, hour after hour.

And there was Pensive, too, and everything
She touched was touched with fear. She married well,
Her people said, but marriage proves a hell
For those who marry but the flesh alone.
Who would have known a turn of mind could bring
Such knowledge to a girl? Who would have known?

I think of her, the child with heavy heart,
Heavy with child, and, Child, I think of you
And all the follies you will journey through;
I know them as an author knows his book.
Action and thought are nothing if apart.
Love in a gesture, wisdom in a look—

These are the real births for which we die.
Outside, the neighbor children startle me,
Calling *Allee, alleeoutsinfree.*
They cut for home. I hear a whirring skate
Fading through the darkness like a sigh.
I dust the frame and set the picture straight.

The Attic

We have ascended to this paradise,
Make-believe angels hurrying to our choirs.
Imagination is our Sunday vice;
We are alone, alone with our desires.

We are enchanted by the sound of rain;
Darkness, half-light, and light combine and blur;
This is the national treasury of Cockaigne,
Of which we are the keepers, as it were.

Time is our Midas. We are of his line;
His touch descends to us on either side
—That golden touch. One gesture will refine
This dust into such realms as dust would hide.

These beads are pearls disguised as imitations.
This broken chair, my dear? It is a throne
From which you may survey the lesser nations,
Those lands that cannot claim you as their own.

This box contains the music of the spheres;
Its Swiss machinery records the stars.
Ever the listener given to fancy hears
The strings of Venus and the drum of Mars.

Time and Imagination—what are they?
They are, my dear, the pseudonyms of Change,
The smooth, indifferent author of our play,
Master of both the common and the strange.

My sister, it is autumn in Cockaigne,
And we are weary, for we've come so far
—Too far to be enchanted by the rain.
We are alone, alone with what we are.

The Junk Shop

The pride of wrights, the joy of smiths abide
        In fallen things—
          In tattered carpetings,
        In blackamoors and chamber pots.
Useless, they stay there in their show of pride
        Under the naked watts.

Is that not childhood in the corner there,
          Color and riot
        So dark now, and so quiet?
        To linger there would be unwise.
What if the tongues of wagons beat the air,
        And dolls opened their eyes?

O milliners, I see you in the hats
          Your deftness made,
        Imprisoned in their shade.
        I mark the cartwheel and the sailor,
The toque, the cloche—these are your habitats,
        Eternity your jailer.

The shoe forsaken is essential last.
          The cobbler fled
        Barefooted with the dead;
        His cunning stayed upon the sole.
Poor boot, your consolation is your past—
        Now broken, you are whole.

Medusa must have looked upon these clocks,
They are so still,
With no time left to kill.
They are like chimneys without lamps,
Or keys forever separate from their locks;
They are like cancelled stamps.

Ah, this is the imperium of things,
Things in themselves.
These crammed and dusty shelves
Contain us in the things we wrought.
These bronze, unbarbered heads are not our kings
But subjects of our thought.

The Black Angel

Where are the people as beautiful as poems,
As calm as mirrors,
With their oceanic longings—
The idler whom reflection loved,
The woman with the iridescent brow?
For I would bring them flowers.

I think of that friend too much moved by music
Who turned to games
And made a game of boredom,
Of that one too much moved by faces
Who turned his face to the wall, and of that marvelous liar
Who turned at last to truth.

They are the past of what was always future.
They speak in tongues,
Silently, about nothing.
They are like old streetcars buried at sea,
In the wrong element, with no place to go. . . .
I will not meet *her* eye,

Although I shall, but here's a butterfly,
And a white flower,
And the moon rising on my nail.
This is the presence of things present,
Where flying woefully is like closing sweetly,
And there is nothing else.

Poem

Let's fly to the famous Asian cities,
Stealing our maps from dark museums,
    Ancient, inaccurate maps
    With curly-headed winds.
Let's fly to the famous Asian cities

On Friday next, at the quitting whistle.
We gather where the road is crooked.
    Our password is your name
    Whatever it may be
On Friday next, at the quitting whistle.

Jews, bindlestiffs, girls with dandruff—
When was there ever a crew so motley?
    How cunning a disguise
    To pass for what we are:
Jews, bindlestiffs, girls with dandruff.

Marvelous animals, beautiful spirits,
We were never much good at being human.
    Like heroes in old films,
    Frantically we flee the world.
Marvelous animals, beautiful spirits!

The Bee-Harp

Winged Victory of Nowhere,
the dressmaker's dummy stood,
guarding the hive in the harp.

Like a string of topaz beads
or a brassy abacus,
the bees flew their sweet missions.

The broken attic window
let them in. A safe distance
away, we watched and wondered.

You seemed intent on the bees,
their dances, how they hovered,
the fingerprints of Midas,

and I thought about the harp,
how it stood in a strange way
for all my lost occasions.

We went downstairs silently,
and made love, and later on
called someone to clean them out.

Doublewalker

You will find me occasionally, there, with you—
the lone shoe in the fast lane
of the freeway, the anonymous key
among your collar studs—
or your hairpins, as the case may be.

I am the factory reject. I inhabit
your daydreams, your nightwatches—
I come on, like something from Dick Tracy.
You have heard the bugles
of the Chinese infantry, perhaps?

I was the bugler. If I bear no resemblance
to my photograph, you know,
nevertheless, the look of me: the dark
mirror calls me Omar,
Omar, and it holds us in its arms.

Once

Remember those gentle kooks
who would stand at the crossroads,
directing traffic, Sundays?

And Grandfather Patterson
in his rocker, whistling down
the beagle in the painting?

And the blind Negress who talked
to herself in a language
all her own, at the corner?

They have disappeared, stealing
the ice cards out of windows,
the cloth fronts of radios.

We tolerated much, once.
Grass grew through our cracked sidewalks,
and the rag man cried and cried.

The Twenty-Fifth Victim

"Dichtenmiller fell asleep, and fell over the tailgate, and was killed by the trailer. He was the twenty-fifth victim of Operation Desert Strike. Today, the mythical armies are inactive."　THE LOS ANGELES TIMES

The mythical armies stall
in the 99°
heat, Private Dichtenmiller,

as if they were mourning you,
young Nod, old Upsy-Daisy,
but that can't be, now can it?

Calonia, Nevona—
neither army can claim you,
or wants to: you were sleeping,

when you became what you dreamed,
became un-American.
The mythical armies rest.

Listen, the dead are singing
the old songs, and telling jokes,
in the dust of Camp Hades.

Cygnets House

This is the last retreat that Graciousness
    Can call her own.
    It stands in brick and stone,
    Victorian to the very eaves,
But for the servants who, I must confess,
    Are bloody modern thieves.

The daughters of the noble and the rich
    Are finished here.
    What polish, what veneer!
    These Helens have their father's nod:
Ledeans know by instinct which is which;
    They know the bill of God.

They learn here what is pleasing to a man.
    From stock exchange
    To modern art they range;
    Of ancient houses, recent horses,
They know the names; and of the Aga Khan,
    The size of his resources.

I ask you, Mrs. Rennie-O'Mahony,
    You, the Queen Swan,
    Inform me if you can
    What cygnets dream of when they sleep.
Is it the wrinkled faces found on money?
    And do the cygnets weep?

Ignore the beggar, kick the sycophant,
I love the class
That paddles on its ass!
The Begum comes, if Aga can;
And if he can't, the Begum speaks of Kant,
Or quotes the Alcoran.

The Fifth Season

It will be summer, spring, or fall—
Or winter, even. Who would know?
For no one answers when we call
Who might have answered years ago.

The harvest will be in or not;
The trees in flower or in rime.
Indifferent to the cold, the hot,
We will no longer care for time.

Mortal, of ivory and of horn,
We will become as open gates
Through which our nothing will be borne,
By which all nothing now but waits.

It will be summer, spring, or fall—
Or winter, even. Who will care?
We will not answer when you call,
For nothing, nothing echoes there.

Elegy for a Secret

You are a mother-in-law
and suffer from hot flashes;
you are an eight-year-old boy
with wide blue eyes and a scar
on your right knee; you are mad
with ambition, and forty,
a man to be counted on.
You are my enemy, O.K.?

You get around. You turn up
in everybody's mirror,
naked. You are a best seller;
the blind are fingering you.
You have become Tchaikovsky;
even the deaf turn you on.
Now you call yourself Scandal
—and sleep with Hyperbole!—

who once lay silent, at ease
in my arms, behind these blinds.
You had only one smile then.
You were, of course, too perfect;
you scared me, and I went out
with you on my arm. Today,
I must mourn a love buried
in the gaze of passers-by.

Life with Mother

Everything's left to the imagination,
Mother says, and winks
an eye, green and beautiful.
I nod encouragement, and wink back,
imagining myself anywhere but here,
in this room, with this woman.

She has been very famous in her lifetimes—
Queen Elizabeth,
Alexander Hamilton—
this poor Irish daughter of the man
who invented the Nabisco fig newton,
this woman who has no friends.

She is being watched by agents of the Kremlin;
an agent herself
of the Ascended Masters,
she knows, she knows. St. Germain is here,
now, in this room. See, the light bulb is blinking!
K-17 is here too,

and the Lord Kathumi is in the kitchen.
I nod, I must nod,
or be a Black Magician.
And if I did speak, what could I say?
There are ashes on all your sidewalks, Mother.
There are ashes in my mouth.

The Sickness of Friends

Do I give off in the wee,
small hours a phosphorescent
glow, perhaps, like rotting wood?

Am I in the Yellow Pages?
I am sick of the sickness
within me that so lures them

to their phones when the night stops
in a dead calm: "H'llo." It's Dick,
who can't bear to be alone;

or Jane, who needs a father;
or Spot, who leads a dog's life.
Even the operator

has twin raw scars on her wrists,
but I'm fine, unmarked, floating
in the bath of their self-love.

Chicken Rampant, Bar Sinister

I tell him my thirteen secret names,
and I say,
"All my decisions are committee decisions,
and some of my selves,
Doctor, are always out of town."

Rich as Onassis, I count my fears.
In my dreams
I see the hard-hearted and familiar strangers
circling around me,
and I don't know if I'm their king

or their victim. Chicken rampant, bar
sinister—
my family coat of arms hangs, invisible,
in an empty room.
Memory's a form of simile:

I am like all my unknown and frightened fathers.

Bitter Suite

I. The Reproach

Observe how life reproaches art:
I, who was lonely in the crowd,
And took my loneliness to heart,
Would now be lonely if allowed.

II. December

Of passion there is little said,
For he would have you think him cold,
Whom passion would not leave for dead,
Though reason found him far too old.

III. Next Question

Oh, who is Goober, what is he?
Inquires the peanut of the pea.
And, thus, the candle to the wick,
Why, Goober, Brightness, is a prick.

IV.   The Gutless Wonder

Dapper I perceive:
Clothes upon a peg:
Nothing up his sleeve,
Nothing down his leg.

V.   Queer at Easy

Where is it that the wise abide?
What houses and what streets are theirs?
Nowhere! Nowhere! The wise have died,
In joy, in silence, without heirs.

VI.   Robert Roger Coulette, Musician

He plays no more
Whose play was need,
The darkened score,
The broken reed.

The Wandering Scholar

The light lies lightly on the leaf;
The rains are fierce and sudden now;
And it is time I packed my books
To go I know not where nor how.

Though scholarship disturbs my brain,
I will not stay where I am put.
Better to go I know not where,
A fever in the better foot.

I curse the libertine of verse
Whose meters lurch when they should tread.
What joy to leave that fool behind,
Wooden ears on a wooden head!

I curse the man who took my style,
The woman who refused her roof.
Better to go—I know not how—
Alone, unsheltered, and aloof.

St. Golias, keeper of my soul,
I seek your footprints in the dust,
And go I know not where nor how,
Unless you answer to my trust,

And bring me through the sudden rain
Into the grove no change can mar,
Where light lies on the laurel leaf,
And bring me where the Muses are.

II   After and Way After

"Poetry is what disappears in translation."

ROBERT FROST

Heredia: Antony and Cleopatra

1

Under the azure where the noon sun totters,
Its golden poop, its silk pavilions
As radiant as a galaxy of suns,
The ship flies in a heaven of blue waters

And from the hawk-like prow receives its name.
Gripping the rail with jewelled hands, she leans
Into the wind: the last of Egypt's queens,
The queen of sparrow-hawks, is out for game.

Here's Tarsus where the Roman Eagle rules
The empty market place; where, Prince of Fools,
Blond Bacchus draws a final, sober breath;

Where maid and eunuch whisper "love and death,"
While Hawk and Eagle grouse and peck and lurch,
Two parakeets upon a single perch.

II

Glare! Shock! and it is done. An officer
Rallies the bronze platoons. The broken air
Echoes their cries and still their nostrils bear
Myrrh from the battlefield, the acrid myrrh.

Eyes of their comrades count the quiet dead.
Now, in the distance, like dead leaves, they see
The archers of Phraortes whirl and flee,
Glistening with sweat, their heads unhelmeted.

Under the floating purple, amid the blare
Of trumpeting monitors and level drums,
The eagles bow and point the way he comes,

Magnificent, reining his frightened mare—
This famous, bleeding Antony for whom
The incandescent sun becomes a plume.

III

The lovers pace the terrace nervously,
See Egypt dream beneath a sultry sky,
And hear the Nile, ambitious serpent, sigh
Through Saïs and Bubastis for the sea.

The Roman feels beneath his stout cuirass—
Captive soldier cradled like a child—
Bending on his triumphant heart, the wild,
Barbaric body golden as his brass.

Winding his white face in her long black hair,
Her body drunk with lust, as light as air,
She offers up her lips and liquid eyes.

The Imperator bends to take his prize,
Sees in those gold-flecked eyes a troubled sea,
Immense and dark, where broken galleys flee.

Catullus: 5

Let's live and love, my Lesbia,
Giving neither hang nor straw
For all the gossip of old men.
The dancing sun will dance again,
But the time comes when we shall be
Wallflowers for eternity,
So *da mi basia,* and then
A hundred thousand times again,
Until no envious bastard knows
What limit envy may impose.

Jaccottet: The Crossing

Beauty in capitals? No!
Landing here at Palermo
in this second-class cabin,
what did I find but beauty,
so lower-case, so common.

The other I saw perhaps
in your face, but our meetings
resembled those enormous
hieroglyphics the moon spells
on the sands south of Naples,

and the moon blots the moon's book.
She is not for the taking.
She never drags an ermine,
evenings, at the casino.
She never answers the phone.

If she were to give herself,
it would only be, I think,
to that most discreet of men,
that inhabitant of dark
corners, the wise wallflower.

III Hermit

"I saw no future in anything."

DENNIS SCOTT FARRELL

1: Evening in the Park

The children have packed up the light
And gone home for the bedtime story
In which Jack wakes the Sleeping Fury.
I count tin cans and comic books;
I listen for the wheel of night,
That furry rim, those velvet spokes.

Some know it by the rush of stars;
I know it by the rush of thought:
Images, like the shrill onslaught
Of cyclists on a black-top road,
Come on and catch me unawares:
I am the victim of their mood.

It is a rehash of the day,
The rooms remembered for their anger,
The crowded stairways for their danger,
And what the light did to a mirror
You thought you knew. It is a way
Of being faithful to one's terror.

I will sit here a little while,
Recalling how I read about
A man who found a strange way out,
The hermit of this wooded park,
Gaunt Crusoe of a nowhere isle,
Who hides his bushel in the dark.

He may be watching even now,
His dark hands up his darker sleeves,
The last of the great make-believes.
He moves in an enormous grave,
The wilderness pressed to his brow,
A man of motion without drive.

I wonder, Does he name the trees?
And to what end? Or like a bird,
Does he know calls that know no word?
And does he conjure without number?
And when, against the moon, he sees
My silhouette, does he remember?

Batman is whispering in the wind;
The cans are jewelled with the stars,
Evening Venus and red-eyed Mars.
I am an eight-hour daylight man,
And I must go to keep my mind
Familiar and American.

2: Elsewhere

I have loved you foolishly, my unaltered
ego, as children
love an invisible friend.
Your Purple Heart and honest parents
were the very things to leave, and if you had
a secret wound, it was

a harbor where the darkness rode at anchor
in imperial calm.
And you had gone; I could stand
on the back porch, the television
voices all around me in the dark, and think
you out there, or mistake

a low star for your campfire, and feel the heat.
Yet, for all I know,
it was I who drew you down,
so friendly, dog-like, among the cops,
the bald psychiatrist, the weeping parents,
the man from Channel 2.

The power of love is spoken of elsewhere.
I note in passing
only how cold the nights are
of late, though, they are not, I suppose,
as cold as the nights you have where they have you,
at home, in Nebraska.

IV The War of the Secret Agents

I gave them bad habits and impossible loves.
I was arrogant,
heavy with ambition, sad.
They were footnotes with beautiful names;
they were passports without photos; they were dust,
and I took that dust in hand.

DRAMATIS PERSONAE

JANE ALABASTER
a scholar who is writing a history
of secret agents
in France during World War II.
She is concerned that many of them
survive only under a cloud of treason.
The lady is a spinster.

PROSPER
the chief of the secret agents in Paris;
captured by Kieffer,
he agrees to a deal whereby,
surrendering his agents, he gains
the promise from Kieffer of their safe-
keeping;
he has a wife named NANCY.

ARCHAMBAULT
He is Prosper's radio operator,
has red hair, very
strange eyes, and writes bad poems.
His Christian name (Gilbert) when
pronounced
in the French manner by Denise rimes
with that
of the following agent:

HILAIRE PENTECÔTE   who bears a most remarkable resem-
                        blance
                    to a famous star
                    of the French screen. Everything
                    passes through his hands, as he is Air
                    Movements Officer for the secret agents.
                    He has no truck with doctors.

DENISE   Prosper's courier and Archambault's
                        mistress,
                    she has a sister,
                    an identical twin named
                    DESIRÉE, who, though not an agent,
                    concerns herself to the point of obses-
                        sion
                    with their comings and goings.

CINEMA, PHONO   These two are among the surviving
                        agents:
                    Cinema the Mad,
                    a rider on the Métro,
                    who becomes a lighthouse keeper; big
                    Phono, a Piccadilly Lazarus, who
                    finds himself—in a tall glass.

BUCKMASTER   the London head of Special Operations
                    Executive (or
                    the S.O.E. or the Firm),
                    an organization consisting
                    of such amateurs as Prosper. BODDING-
                        TON
                    is his second in command.

[54]

THE GERMANS   KIEFFER, the head of the Paris Gestapo,
who kept his promise
as long as promises could
be kept; WULF, his second in command,
who ends as a mental patient; and
YEAGER,
a member of the *Wehrmacht*.

THE OTHERS   MAMA BEE is a famous American
medium who tries
to contact Prosper. MADAME
GUEPIN, an ex-Resistance member.
THE ABBÉ OF ARDON, a scholar. T.S.
ELIOT, an editor.

1. Proem

Prosper, Archambault, Gilbert, and Cinema—
romantic code-names
out of a teen-age novel
(The Motor Boys and the Gestapo)—
who can remain unmoved at the wedding
of youth and propaganda?

And so with their transmitters they came to France,
gifted amateurs
ready to die for England
and the S.O.E. How could they know
that what London told them was a nightmare
London had from Hollywood?

They will appeal to lovers of the absurd:
there they were, bulging
with codes and automatics.
Like debutantes slumming on Skid Row,
they couldn't be missed—they advertised
and Death reads all the papers.

II. *Jane Alabaster: A Letter to T.S. Eliot*

Dearest Possum,

                    It is as if I wrote you
not from this Paris,
the capital of the Franks,
but from another, from a city
thrice more ancient, where gargoyles lean and leer
from parapets more subtle,

the ultimate prospect, ultimate Paris.
The quest is over!
Now the last chapter: Gilbert
has promised to meet me—"to explain"—
as if explanation were still possible.
Now to confront him at last!

Do you realize I have spent some five years
with the words of ghosts,
in the company of men
who, if they were not ghosts, were more mad,
more broken than we imagine men can be
and still be men and not ghosts?

The quest is over, with what joy! what sadness!
Five years of my life
in order to crown my life—
well, surely, it was worth it, Possum.
Faber and Faber, you shall have your manuscript,
And I shall have my laurels—

and what laurels, too! for my text is human.
I have established
the reading of what moves,
breathes, and has known too much suffering.
Forgive me, dear friend, if I brag a little.
Tomorrow I am forty

and tomorrow in the Place de la Concorde
I will meet Gilbert;
and meeting him, I will count
forty not as lonely women do
but as poets count their strophes, with a sense
of the timeless and the true.

III. Anonymous: On a Wall at Buchenwald

11 November 1944—
I had one motive,
comfort, and I ended up
on a cold floor. I had one virtue,
loyalty, and I carried it far too far.
Goodbye, Goldilocks. Goodbye.

IV. Kieffer's Diary: 1942–45: Excerpts [1]

1.

It is like a musical composition
without music, pure
as music can never be,
or a monstrous, new form of blindfold
chess, where the moves are all Byzantine, unknown.
Am I mad from paper-work?

2.

I find myself indifferent to places.
Paris means nothing;
Germany is forgotten.
I care only for the quirks of men.
Indeed, I study even the guards: brute Slavs,
dim Rumanian lackeys.

[1] *S.S. Sturmbannführer Hans Otto Kieffer*
counted beautiful
women, good food, and sports cars
among his passions, yet this diary,
found after his execution, indicates
a man of more than passion.

3.

What a beautiful, evil son of a bitch
Gilbert proves himself!
Photostats of Prosper's
reports to London clutter my desk.
He writes with such style that my English improves
Is there a style for pity?

4.

I begin to know Prosper and his comrades.
There are even times
when I can sense their terror;
it is as though I were watching, too,
gazing up at my own office, at this light,
myself gazing at myself.

5.

What was an amusement is now a danger.
Africa, Russia—
what I delayed must begin:
we will come in the night like bad dreams.
I look forward to meeting them, as I might
the authors of my childhood.

6.

Name: Francis Suttill alias Prosper;
name: Gilbert Norman
alias Archambault; name:
Andrée Borrel alias Denise—
the shepherd has been introduced to his flock.
How shall I use my poor sheep?

7.

A long talk with Prosper—I have given him
my formal promise:
no harm will come to his men,
none at all, if he cooperates.
He is as honest as a cavalryman;
London has sent me a child.

8.

We two are caught up in a dream of pity.
We sit together
nodding over his reports,
his letters to his wife. Sleepwalker,
London was your God, and God has betrayed you.
You have my word, my pity.

9.

He consents!

10.

We have bagged over a thousand.
They are in the net,
and not one drop of blood spilt.
What a beautiful, evil Gilbert—
to have given me so many charming birds,
to have given me their songs!

11.

A little treatise on the uses of song,
on the radio game?
London responds, arming us.
Yes, yes, they are sending us arms,
and I am sending messages to their wives.
Dear God, the uses of song!

12.

London has sent us a Major Boddington,
whom we wined and dined
and sent back in ignorance;
four commandoes whom we had to kill.
So blood has been spilt, so I must ask myself,
How can we lose? and still lose.

13.

Wulf and I have been trying to burn records;
there are too many.
And my lost sheep, where are they?
Exhausted beyond caring, we laugh,
hearing the festival of guns in the street,
in the Bois de Boulogne.

14.

They say I am to be hanged. I don't know why.
The four commandoes?
No, it is that they fear me,
that they fear what I don't know I know.
They fear what I might say, yet I would not speak:
the methods . . . the methods go on. . . .

V. *Notes on the Backs of Envelopes*

1. Colonel Buckmaster

Truth, madam, is a waif in the wilderness—
it dies of neglect.
We have chosen to forget,
deliberately, out of kindness.
Truth is, Archambault was the English Judas
we have chosen to forget.

2. Colonel Yeager

The retreat from Paris was an Olympics
for half-mad cripples.
We limped and raved across France,
the great jaw of Chaos at our heels.
Germany had no time for Kieffer's promise;
she was preparing to die.

3. Madame Guepin

Denise in the prison at Fresnes told me,
—*Gilbert me protège.*
She told me this, yes, and this,
—*C'est Gilbert qui nous a tous vendus.*
The dead are dead, and we live out the new lies,
without love, beyond betrayal.

VI. A Page from an Official History by the
    Abbé of Ardon

Her sister, hearing of her imprisonment,
confronted the Boche
and begged to be made captive,
though innocent of Denise's crime.
Whatever their motive, they complied.
The Lord have mercy on her.

They came finally to the Natzweiler Camp,
where the sick were gassed,
and her sister being ill,
Denise begged to be chosen as well.
Thus, these daughters of France came to embrace Death.
The Lord have mercy on them.

VII. *Cinema, at the Lighthouse*

I admire the driven, those who rise from choice
as from a sick bed.
I was of that company,
as you are, as he is whom you seek.
What little I know you must know, or have guessed.
Prosper, I assume, is dead;

we last met beside the train that had brought us
into Germany.
We came upon each other
in the steam of the brakes, and his eyes
were those of a blindman or a cuckold. We passed
each other without speaking.

The other one I met once on an airfield
my first night in France.
If I remember rightly,
we did not speak; perhaps we nodded;
perhaps his hand touched my elbow. I recall
only the scent of the cut hay

and the overwhelming sensual delight
I knew momently
under the dangerous moon.
Your prey was of the breathing darkness
wherein, without father, Cinema was born—
he was midwife at that birth.

A ghost of a cockney with a gift of tongues,
what did I become?
Whatever Cinema did,
and he did it well. And when I slept,
I could hear the nations underneath my ear,
and my dreams were of pure light.

This has the ring of nonsense about it, no?
How can I tell you?
How can I explain to one
never there? I was a courier
and rode the Métro, disguised differently
everyday. I was no one,

I was what I seemed, I did not have to think.
This house is the grave
of Cinema, and this light
his epitaph. How can I explain
the dead? The dead are an extravagant cheese,
nor have the sad gift of tongues.

VIII. *Mama Bee, the Famous American Medium,*
    Tries to Contact Prosper

The right frame of mind, honey, is a calm hope,
what Daddy Bee calls
"A Gentle Expectancy."
It's the practical approach to faith.
Now, my guide's a little Spanish spirit named
Guadalupe—you'll like her.

Let's begin . . . Guadalupe, Guadalupe,
can you hear me, dear?
Guadalupe, can you hear?
Am I getting through to you, honey?
We are trying to contact Major Suttill,
Major Francis Suttill, dear.

—*¿Como esta, Mama? ¿Que pasa? ¿Subtle who?*
No, Guadalupe,
it's Major Francis Suttill;
we think he passed over in the war.
Do you know him, honey, in the Great Beyond?
Honey, do you know him there?

(I am here. I wear the mufti of a shade.)
Is he there, honey?
Am I getting through to you?
(Mufti, and memory like a chain . . .)
Guadalupe, Guadalupe, are you there?
—*Vaya con Dios, Mama.*

IX. Denise: A Letter Never Sent

Desirée,
            I find it most bitter that you,
my sister, my twin,
should set your heart against me.
Gilbert is my love, my protection—
I am no streetwalker in a scarlet sheath
tripping through the Place Pigalle.

How stupid, how petite-bourgeoise to unleash
such rabid, convent-
bred imaginings upon
me—your own sister, your twin!
I had thought to share the sweetness of my love.
How carefully I chose words!

I wanted so to tell you of this strange gift,
for I must conceive
of love as something given—
I wanted to tell you of Gilbert,
of how he crams my very being with such love,
and of his marvelous eyes.

Now you have come between me and my mirror.
How can I behold
my image—yes, our image—
without rancor? I must school myself
to be an only child, beyond reflection,
marvelous to his marvelous eyes.

X. *Archambault: A Suspicious Poem*

The lost addresses of the soul are these:
the great estate
with mermaids at the gate
or the cold-water flat with wolves—
wherever loneliness like a disease
or a wildflower evolves—

or where like alabaster in the dark
she lies in wait
whom you would celebrate
in the exclusion of the mind,
whom you, in dreams, inchoate, know as ark,
crucible, and rind—

or where, powerful, irresponsible,
you turn away
from what the others say,
and—like a mirror come to life—
make of duplicity the single rule,
and use it like a knife.

XI. Orphan Annie: The Broken Code

8-9-12-1-9-18-5-16-5
14-20-5
3-15-20-5-9
19-1-4-15-21
2-12-5-1-7-5-14-20-6
15-18-11 . . .

XII. *Phono, at the Boar's Head*

Thanks, I will.

                You understand he wasn't mad?
even in the end?
Oh, I was there, I saw him,
I saw his mind become more lucid
hour by hour, thought by thought, lucid as the flesh
of the old, the very old,

a Chinese wisdom. I give you the Chinese.
I give you nothing
you can't find out for yourself,
except the last look of Archambault:
the delicate, livid face of a red-head,
with one brown eye, and one blue.

We knew at Mauthausen that we were to die.
My fear kept me sane;
I talked to it in my head.
Show these bastards how to die, I said.
My days were like dreams, in which I dreamt my death,
and lived like a coward.

And all the while Archambault lay there smiling
like a god damn saint.
There is nothing left to lose,
he said. *Nothing but my frigging life,*
I said, but he didn't hear me, or he heard
and knew there was nothing left.

[74]

Did you know, he laughed, *they captured us in bed,*
in Denise's bed?
I woke up with their torches
in my face. I dreamed they would be there,
and they were, and I wasn't afraid. I sighed,
I think, with satisfaction.

I rose, I stood stock still. I read the letter-
ing on the light bulb.
I saw Denise's nipples,
taut, purple, oddly oval. I heard
the embarrassed creaking of the German coats.
I smelled the oil on their guns

I saw the world, and I gave back what I saw.
I was a mirror,
nothing more. I was faithful;
I gave an eye for an eye. Can they
execute a mirror? There will be gunfire
and an end to reflection.

—Show these Gothic bastards how to die, I said.
—You show them, he said,
and don't forget to say "cheese."
—Fuck your brown eye, and your blue, I said,
and in the morning, the guards took him outside
and shot him, and I waited,

knowing I would be next, saying, *Show them how* . . .
I waited nine months,
and the Americans came.
It was 80 days before I walked.
I was Lazarus come to Piccadilly,
unseeing, among strangers,

among the accusing Buckmasters of London,
among the whispers
of *treason, treason.*—*Bad show,*
a bad show best forgotten, old man,
Buckmaster said. He was embarrassed for me;
I had neglected to die.

It's madness, I know, but they wanted us dead.
Are the files neater
if you die? What Prosper did
when he dickered with that German crank
was to save a few lives—oh, not the best lives,
but a few; that was his crime.

And when you ask me why I drink, I must say
I don't know. Is it
in memory of Prosper,
of silly Prosper? Do I follow
Archambault by fifths, a brown eye, and a blue?
The Buckmasters of this world—

do I drink to stomach them? Or the coward
who waited nine months
and the Americans came?
Well, I give you the Americans.
Now one more for the road, and do count your change;
the publican is a cheat.

XIII. *Buckmaster on the BBC*

The rose is more than a handful of petals;
the hive is greater
than the meandering bee.
We are moved by, and toward, absolutes:
the rose for meaning, and the hive for purpose.
The rose, the hive, and Special

Operations Executive—or The Firm,
as we called it then—
what do they have in common?
Well, what is bravery without a cause?
How could any one of us fall asleep nights
without the rose and the hive?

XIV. Wulf, at the Asylum

The doctors regard me as a classic case,
and that's the story
that I've doctored up for them,
or you, or any who come rooting
among my hems and haws. I'm a specialist;
I prescribe what you ask for,

and you ask for Kieffer. How will you have him?
wriggling on a rope?
or alone, the middle-aged
dandy, mooning over a desk lamp?
Kieffer, you know, could never cross his ankles
for fear of spoiling his shine:

we Germans have been seduced by our tailors.
We move, when we march,
in an ecstasy of tabs
and ribbons—the beautiful soldiers! [2]
So Kieffer sat there at his great cherry desk,
his ankles never touching;

[2] *It must be noted that the speaker was not*
   himself a soldier,
   for he belonged, like Kieffer,
   his superior, to the Gestapo,
   though that organization was properly
   known as the Sicherheitsdienst.

behind him, on the wall, framing his heavy,
military head,
the yellow map of Paris,
the tacks glistening like caught insects.
Gilbert stood among the shadows in the office,
and the shadows were like dark

angels landing and taking off. They whispered,
Gilbert and Kieffer,
or was it the sound of wings?
Desirée had turned against Denise,
as sisters turn against sisters in a world
carnivorous, but Kieffer

would delay, admiring his boots, and the tacks
glistened all night long.
Desirée was so lovely,
I could not believe she had a twin,
that that dark hair, those lost eyes, that crooked mouth
had any equals ever.

So Desirée came to Kieffer now and then,
and Kieffer would smile
as a parent smiles, hearing
a good lesson, and send her away.
This all happened a long time ago, and we
have all died, this way or that.

XV. *Prosper: A Letter to Nancy* [3]

Le Sacré-Coeur trembles on the window pane,
a lorry rumbles
down the street, a baby cries
somewhere below stairs—who was it said,
Paris is for Englishmen and pickpockets;
lovers go to the country?

I am having one of my headaches today.
In a few minutes
the others will start arriving:
lumbering Phono, mad Cinema,
and the star-crossed lovers, of course. I must play
the greybeard for these children.

[3] *Nancy Suttill has remarried. Her husband*
is a car salesman
in Leeds. They have two children,
a daughter and an adopted son;
the son has been named Prosper—Prosper
Pulkinghorn, to be exact.

It is Nancy Pulkinghorn who has observed
that this strange letter
may be the work of Kieffer
(see Section Eleven of Part Four).
At this late date, she is unable to say
more than this on this matter.

Their reports, as usual, will be worthless.
The Jerry troop train
is late. It is! It isn't!
But no, it has already arrived.
And then the arguments will start. Cinema
will storm out. Denise will cry.

When my cigarettes are gone, and my patience,
why, then they will leave,
and I will peer down at them,
there, on the street, and I will whisper,
God damn you, God damn you, I'm through, I've had it,
I'm going home to Nancy!

Then, I'll look around the room and see the flowers
Denise has brought me
for my desk. I'll arrange them,
giving them water, knowing I'll stay.
It is the thought of you that keeps me going,
but this is the way I go.

XVI. *Hilaire Pentecôte, His Horoscope*

They were at a corner table in the Ritz.
Jean Gabin, she thought;
He looks just like Jean Gabin.
Hilaire had removed his dark glasses,
and his eyes were both wary and amused.
"You are Gilbert," she stated.

"No, I was Gilbert. I am Hilaire Pentecôte.
They are but two names
among many. There are names
on every side, waiting to be used;
I help myself. But what is it that you want?"
"You are Gilbert," she answered.

"I want justice. I confront you with your past."
"Ah, my dear lady,
you want justice in the Ritz?"
He made a soft gesture, and his hand
described the four-star luxury of the room.
"There were two of you," she said;

"The English Gilbert and the French Gilbert.
You are the latter,
the one of whom Denise said,
'C'est Gilbert qui nous a tous vendus.'
You sold them out, and a dead man got the blame."
"You are absolutely right,"

he said. "But what of it? What is it to you?"
"Just this," she answered:
"it wasn't Gilbert Norman,
and it wasn't that poor demented
girl, Desirée, either. My book will clear them."
"And label me a traitor?"

"Yes." "No," he answered; "that isn't possible."
"But it is. I can . . ."
"No," and he smiled; "no, you can't,
for I'm not the traitor that you think."
"But they gave the papers to you for the planes,
and you gave them to Kieffer,

"and Kieffer copied them, and gave them back . . ."
She was breathless now,
frightened by the innocence
that rode upon his smile. "Yes," he said,
"but I did only what London told me to—
I was London's instrument.

"There was an underground beneath the underground.
They protected it.
Kieffer never guessed the truth;
he was too busy counting the sheep
London let him have by way of sacrifice—
fifteen hundred little lambs!"

"No," she murmured, but she knew he spoke the truth.
It was as if truth
had an odor about it,
distinct, acrid as a camphor lamp.
"How do I know," she asked, "that you are not telling me an enormous lie?"

"You don't," he answered, and then he laughed. "Do you
    think
London will confirm
what I whisper in the Ritz?
No, but you can prove me innocent.
Write your book, and see if London prosecutes:
London will not lift a hand."

"Dear God," she said; "it is all too horrible:
fifteen hundred lives!"
"Yes," he said and touched her hand.
"It was no business for angels,
or sheep, or an Ivanhoe like our Prosper.
I am a religious man,

"and it grieves me." He said this almost shyly.
She looked at Hilaire.
"You have then a religion?"
"Yes," he said. "May I ask what it is?"
"Christian Science," he answered in a fine confusion.
"I am interested myself,"

she said, "in astrology. May I ask you
your chronology?
I have an ephemeris
in my bag." She took it from her purse.
"September 2, 1909,
at eleven in the night."

As he sipped his drink, a black currant syrup,
she drew a rough chart
on the back of the wine list.
"Your horoscope," she said, "is under
the dominance of an almost exactly
rising Neptune, and Neptune

"implies a taste for adventure—on all planes,
and in all senses,
embracing on the one hand
an aspiration toward the mystical,
and on the other, the mundane, a penchant
toward secret activities,

"with a liability toward duplicity.
I beg your pardon,
but it's here your drama lies,
especially as your planet's caught up
in a most spectacular grand-cross,
and a grand-cross, my dear sir,

"demands a working out in terms of violence."
He clutched the wine list
to him. "Now that," he said, "that
is fascinating. I mean really."
She smiled and nodded, and they sat silently
till the waiter brought the check.

XVII. Epilogue: Author to Reader

Reader, we are getting ready to pull out.
Archambault has packed
the transmitter in an old
suitcase. Denise is combing her hair.
We are meeting Phono and Cinema downtown
in a second-rate bistro.

Prosper has been worrying about Phono;
he has a bad cough.
—And Cinema, I worry
about Cinema, who must insist
on a trenchcoat, of all things. But life goes on,
even here, in its own way.

Reader, you have been as patient as an agent
waiting at midnight
outside a deserted house
in a cold rain. You will ask yourself,
What does it all mean? What purpose does it serve,
my being here in this rain?

Reader (you will be known henceforth by that name),
there is no meaning
or purpose; only the codes.
So think of us, of Prosper, silly
Prosper, of Archambault of the marvelous eyes,
of Denise combing her hair.

V   Moby Jane

"In Piccadilly
  there lived a kid
  who picked a lily
  a lily he did
  a golden-flowered lily
  a lilac, and his nose."

GLEN MILLER EPSTEIN

The Academic Poet

My office partner dozes
at his desk, whimpering now
as he dreams his suicide.
The November light kisses
the scar of his last attempt.
I open my mail: a plea
for the starving Indian
children of North Dakota;

a special offer from *Time,*
Life, and *Fortune;* a letter
from a 65-year-old
former student, suggesting
a gland transplant that will make
a man of me: it hurts him
to hear what they are saying
about me behind my back.

It hurts me to hear what they
are saying to my face, pal.
I circle two misspelled words
and write, "Help, I am being
held captive at Mickey Mouse
State College," across the top,
wondering, is this the one,
or the fat woman, perhaps,

with the post-menopause craze
for strict forms. "The sestina—
can you use any six words?"
Well, yes, but they should define
a circle, which is the shape
I describe, chasing my tail
from class to class, the straight line
disguised, degree by degree.

The Blue-Eyed Precinct Worker

Liberal, blue-eyed, shivering, trying not
to look like a bill
collector or detective,
I move through the slums in a drizzle—
the slums of Pasadena, where—nutmeg, bronze,
and purple—the Negroes live.

They look out and laugh—Mrs. Bessie Simpson,
Miss Delilah Jones,
the eleven Tollivers.
They are extras in a bad movie
starring no one they have ever seen before,
no one that they care to know.

I am like a man rich in the currency
of a lost kingdom,
for this both is and is not
what I sought. Somewhere, a screen door bangs
and bangs, but in the half-light I can't see where,
or give the sound direction.

A black and white sausage of a mongrel bitch
follows me, sniffing;
her obscene stump of a tail
motionless. We go, the two of us,
to the muddy edge of the dark arroyo.
The street light blooms overhead;

our shadows burst forth monstrous and alien.
There, on the far rim,
are the houses of the rich.
It is the dinner hour, and they eat
prime rib of unicorn, or breast of phoenix.
It is another precinct.

Oddly enough, I am consoled by the thought
of the delicate
small animals that move down
through the arroyo: white coyote,
masked coon, and the plumed skunk. Come, Citizen Dog,
we have chosen the short straw.

At the Telephone Club

We sit, crookbacked, at the bar,
each with his own telephone,
all of us with the same itch.
The tight-assed operator
in the opera stockings
—the only one worth having—
hovers, wisely, out of reach.
She has got all our numbers.

My phone rings: it's the matron
with lost eyes and a horse jaw.
I get rid of her: I have
an ugliness within me,
whole as I am not, a kind
of sleeping cancer. Who needs more?
I listen to the broken
English of an Amsterdam

blonde, seduced in her twelfth year—
it was summer!—by a man
in a Silver Cloud, but I
can have her now for the price
of a taxi ride. I can
have her in a Murphy bed,
while the roaches on the sink
stiffen their fine antennae.

I would, I would, dear lady,
but I have a plane to catch,
one piloted by a sly
Tibetan. I have a date
with some porters in the snow.
I buy her a Grasshopper,
and slip out into the night.
How cold the stars are, how clear!

Table Fourteen

He lay there, our Babe Ruth, in a plastic bag.
We opened the bag.

The skin is leather, the color of Playdough,
And it is cold.

The hair has been removed with a blowtorch,
Which leaves no marks.

We will not be working on the extremities
For some time,

So we smear them—the head, the hands, and the feet—
With Vaseline,

(In the left temple, there is a bullet hole;
On the right, a bruise)

And we wrap them—the extremities—in white muslin
To preserve them.

We have noticed, as we smear the Vaseline,
The strange resemblance

To the King of Swat, who hit sixty home runs
The year I was born.

. . . We're on the chest, removing the fat, which looks
Like scrambled eggs,

When they give us another, a newcomer, an infant,
Still-born and green,

We put it, the babe, with the Babe's heart and lungs,
Between his legs.

Lines for LBG-30, Computer, Poet

So there you are in Glendale,
your circuits open and hot,
your dials iridescent—

the pure poet breaking through,
into pure nonsense, your own
tenth muse, inhuman, perfect.

I must envy you, for see
how this hand trembles among
these half-finished, abandoned

odes, how migraine dulls the eye
that looks on them. If sometimes
my worksheets stir and blossom,

airborne, they do so only
in that odd, recurring dream
wherein I dream my dying,

and see the whole world file past,
forgiving me, blessing me—
my mad mother, my good wife,

the poets I've stolen from,
the interminable strangers.
Dreamless, you go on and on.

If I feed you my sick lines,
will your indifference clean
and polish and complete them?

White Slip, White Shoes

Her laughter is like crystal on a crowded shelf—
this woman in the white slip,
this girl in the white shoes; and her right arm
is a moon journeying,
a half-moon combing the long darkness.

Wantonness is made of olives and the crushed rose.
I have lifted, with these hands,
her ass, magnificent to the catlight,
and Omar in his tower
knew no burden half so sweet, poor guy!

Even Now

The whites of your eyes are blue,
and you show them, evading
my comic, desperate look.

Your nipples are soft, even
now as you come, and you come
so softly, without shudder,

without moan, that I must wait
the coming of your boredom,
and that sigh, before I know.

I am like a stranger, cold
at daybreak, and you are like
a sleeping house, warm and locked.

Mine

Surrounded by ancient *Life*s,
chainsmoking, playing the role
I have come here not to play,

I think what a good poem
this will make, a modern one,
something suited to my style.

I store up details: fumbling
the five bills into the small
envelope delicately

handed to me, my quick check
of those hands to see they're clean,
his fifteen-minute story

of how he came to do time,
and is just out, how the place
may be bugged, how detectives

may approach me when I leave.
He goes back to her. Later,
she will tell me how he cleaned

the previous spring's birds' nests
from the air conditioner,
and chatted, while she rested;

and as she talks, I will be
surprised by my innocence,
and feel it die, and feel old.

Conceived in love and anger,
your dark mother crying, No!
what were you but a tiny

fist of blood that should have beat
against doors till one opened
and your father took you in?

Now you are these lines, these lines
I cannot put my name to,
or make good enough to live.

S-F

Because you had asked for your innocence,
I turned back all the clocks of the world.
I shall remember my work a long time.

I saw the dead man take back his will,
And the infant become an echo and fade.
I saw my best poems die.

Now it is the day before yesterday,
And we are made of politeness and distance.
How odd, our not knowing each other,

For the world seems somehow smaller.
Stranger, were you what you were,
You would be wearing it in your hair.

Thimble City

"Anything can happen in Thimble City,
because you run it."—ad for a Remco toy

A filling station, a car,
a skyscraper, and a house—
that's enough for any town.

The car, full of gasoline,
goes a hundred miles an hour,
but no one ever drives it.

Where's to go? The skyscraper
has a poet in every room,
and each poet is a school

unto himself. And the house?
The house is where the lovers
(meaning you, meaning me) live.

It is where we never hurt
each other, and is no place
I have been to or heard of.

An American Affair

On the headboard of a bed
he'd never get her into,
he inscribed her secret name

No one knows the name for sure.
America, Moby Jane,
and *Wilderness* are good bets.

She was like a promised land:
you can guess the fantasies
he had about getting there.

And it's true, too, that his eyes
had the look, findrinny, glazed,
of one who pursues a beast.

She was like a wilderness,
a tolerance of madness
where he could become himself.

He slept in that bed alone,
profoundly, as a worker
sleeps who can count on his job—

so profoundly rich men wept,
dreaming the dreams their poor wives
wanted frocks the colors of.

Moby Jane

He was a terrible man!
All those dim, useless scribblings
on a beast none had sighted,

except, perhaps, in his smile,
that secret, embarrassed smile.
Was he all he said he was?

Probably. The manuscript—
if you could call it that, that
swelling of black bedabbled

leaves, that pasting together
of odd thoughts, dark reflections—
the manuscript was the beast.

He was something else again.
Not that we thought of signing
the necessary papers;

that would be playing his game,
the nib on the dotted line,
the beast among us, spuming!

Last Effects

He was one of us, surely,
for look what we have found here
in the corners where he lived:

unpaid bills, pornographic
playing cards, six love letters
with circles over the i's.

He pretended otherwise:
the photograph of Baudelaire,
the Burberry, the XK-E.

But there were times, and I speak
perhaps only personally,
when everything coalesced—

one time, we had been drinking
Chivas Regal all that night,
and the eucalyptus burned

in the fireplace, and the dawn,
or the false dawn—whichever
it was—lighted the hawk home,

he said, *When I have kicked off*
and they cut me open, they
will find a dime-store diamond,

worthless, but reflecting light
where the heart is said to be.
And when we cut, we found it.

Notes

Either in time or manner, the poems of the first section are early. The order of the other sections is simply chronological.

The penultimate line of "The Black Angel" is from a poem by LBG-30.

One-third of "The Sickness of Friends" is the work of Philip Levine.

"The War of the Secret Agents" is based on Jean Overton Fuller's remarkable *Double Webs*.

The penultimate line of the penultimate stanza of "The Blue-Eyed Precinct Worker" is from a mystery by Ross Macdonald.